MW01282619

LAYERS OF HEALING

Discovering Purpose in Pain and Trauma

CHANTAEU MUNROE

LAYERS OF HEALING. Copyright © 2024. Chantaeu Munroe. All Rights Reserved.

Printed in the United States of America.

No portion of this book may be reproduced, stored in a retrieval system, or transmitted in any form or by any means, except for brief quotations in printed reviews, without the prior written permission of DayeLight Publishers or Chantaeu Munroe.

ISBN: 978-1-958443-83-5 (paperback)

Scripture quotations marked "KJV" are taken from the Holy Bible, King James Version (Public Domain).

Scripture quotations taken from the Amplified® Bible (AMP). Copyright © 2015 by The Lockman Foundation. Used by permission. www.Lockman.org.

"And we know [with great confidence] that God [who is deeply concerned about us] causes all things to work together [as a plan] for good for those who love God, to those who are called according to His plan and purpose." (Romans 8:28 - A.M.P.).

This book is dedicated to all the women who will read this book and find their way to God. There is hope on the other side of your pain, there is freedom that can be found on the other side of that fear, and there is divine joy that can be discovered because of facing your pain and trauma head-on.

ACKNOWLEDGMENTS

My journey in completing this book was made possible through the invaluable coaching and support provided by DayeLight Publishers, particularly by my dedicated book coach, Crystal Daye. Her guidance during the Reach Millions Author Accelerator over four months was instrumental in bringing this book to life. When it came to editing, designing, marketing, and publishing, her company served as a comprehensive solution, making the entire process seamless and rewarding.

I am deeply grateful to God for His support and guidance throughout this endeavor, allowing me to birth this book and establish a legacy for future generations.

To my mother, Staysie Spence, for demonstrating to me from very early what it means to be resilient in the face of adversity.

To my church family at Church on the Rock, Kingston, who guided me on the path of healing and deliverance, especially teaching me how to hone the gifts that God has trusted me with, which have become instrumental on this journey of purpose.

I extend my heartfelt thanks to all who chose to purchase and read this book. I hope the insights and guidance contained within these pages will empower you to lead a healthier, healed, and purposeful life.

TABLE OF CONTENTS

INTRODUCTION

Christian, unmarried and pregnant—with twins. *The consequences of disobeying God,* I said to myself.

My body was still producing the hCG (Human chorionic gonadotropin) hormone that confirmed I was still pregnant, and at the same time, there was deadness in my womb due to a missed miscarriage, or some call it a silent miscarriage or missed abortion. As a Christian, I had no business having sex—unprotected sex at that—so what did I expect was going to happen?

To make matters worse, God did warn me repeatedly, but I didn't listen. Now there I was: I lost my twins, lost my relationship, and I was about to lose my mind. No one told me that this was normal, and I was not alone. My journey with pain and trauma compounded.

To be honest, my journey has felt like an "on-the-job training" from as far back as seven years old. Who would have thought that all the hell I managed to scrape through was preparing me for such a time as this, that I would have made it on the other side filled with unexplainable joy that surpasses all understanding?

Keep going!

I am now on the other side of fear, exercising faith and showing up pumped with hope each day as a trauma coach and the C.E.O. and founder of C.K.M. Healing Consultancy. With a daily dose of yes in obedience to God, I am on a mission to reach people who are broken to inspire hope in their lives and to demonstrate that with a little care, together, we can help to kindle the mind for healing.

This book is for the woman who is crippled by pain from the trauma she has experienced to teach her how to face her pain, dive deep into the layers of her trauma to bring healing, transformation, and God's perfect purpose out of her. I include my own story of healing and transformation, providing a guide with the tools for healing and deliverance.

In the layers of this book, you will find parts of my story, prayer, and journal prompt exercises to help you begin your journey of healing literally and practically. To top it off, we provide the support you need to take the journey.

You are not alone. Keep going.

CHAPTER ONE

THE DAY PAIN SAID HELLO

In all my years of experiencing pain, I had never felt pain quite like this. The earth stood still. What felt like an 8.5 magnitude earthquake in my abdomen had just passed through my body. Immediately, I had to be rushed home and taken to the bathroom and, to my surprise, the remnants of the surgery I had done four weeks prior showed up. The surgery I did reminded me that I had just lost twins. It was no fault of my own because apparently, these things happen—or so I found out after the fact—but at that moment, the reality hit; I felt worthless. At that moment, I felt like God had made a mistake, and everything that was supposed to make sense suddenly made no sense. My tummy was in a knot; my heart began pounding, and the pain from what I was experiencing silenced everything around me. There was a sound of nothingness.

Pains Unexpected Visit: A Wake-Up Call!

In 2016, I was in a relationship I had no business being in. I was in a relationship that was failing but because I had invested so much, I was convinced that he was my person and no one, not even God, could tell me otherwise. We tried not to have sex for a year but then came January 2017. I had a dream that I was pregnant with twins, and in the dream, I took them out and placed them on a white towel. I had called my boyfriend at the time to tell him we had lost the babies and, in the dream, I was asking myself, *"Who calls their partner and tells them with such excitement that we have lost the babies?"* I woke up from the dream. I didn't think anything of it at the time. I didn't understand how God spoke to me, or I underestimated how God spoke, so life continued after I woke up.

Three months down the line in that same year, I had another dream. This dream was different. It was very specific and detailed. This dream depicted me in the bathroom of my grandmother's house in the States with a digital pregnancy test in my hand that said pregnant. I remember the color of my nails, the time of day, and the color of the clothes I was wearing; I remembered every detail. Again, I didn't take the dream seriously. I thought the dream had nothing to do with me. Later that same year, I started to have sex—a lot—with my Christian boyfriend.

As Christians, we tend to forget that we are human beings who have urges and desires. We are imperfect beings trying to do the right thing. That year, in November, I traveled. I was feeling queasy; typical feelings of pre-period symptoms (P.M.S.), so I thought of it as nothing. I thought my period was coming, and it was time to prepare.

The relationship was falling apart; it was on the verge of snapping and God was showing me all the reasons why I needed to let go of the relationship because He had work for me to do. But I still held on tightly as if somehow, I was entitled to it. So, I traveled, and while traveling, I realized my period didn't come. I thought maybe because I was having sex, my hormones were out of whack, so my period was late because of those recent activities. I didn't think I was pregnant, or maybe I was lying to myself. Sometimes, we know the truth because our bodies speak to us as females, but I convinced myself that I was not pregnant. But I felt like deep down, I knew.

I started to have food aversions. I didn't throw up, but everything suddenly made me nauseous. I decided to go to the pharmacy one day. It was a few blocks down from my grandparents' house. I went as discreetly as I could because I didn't want my family to know I might be pregnant. I got three different tests. I went to the bathroom, tried the first one; the two lines showed up,

13

which meant pregnant. In disbelief, I tried the next one and it said pregnant; the third and final one confirmed the first two. I was PREGNANT! As I sat there, I heard a ringing in my ears, and everything became silent. I looked at the test results and started to get chills. My hands were trembling. I thought to myself, *"O.M.G.! This is happening. I am pregnant. O.M.G.!"* I was in the bathroom looking at the test and freaking out. I remembered the dream I had earlier in the year, which was very detailed. That moment felt like a deja vu moment. I was pregnant!

In November 2017, it was time to go back home from my trip overseas. When I got home, I went straight to my gynecologist, who confirmed the pregnancy—TWINS! Two heartbeats. I was there with my boyfriend at the time; excited, anticipation, family members were excited, my boyfriend was excited. I wasn't sure how I felt, but everyone around us was excited.

One night, not long after—I was about seven weeks at this point heading into eight weeks pregnant with twins—I can't remember the exact reason, but I asked, and my boyfriend's friends took me to the hospital. I was not ill, and neither was I in pain, but I could tell something wasn't right; there was a stillness in me. I went to the hospital at 3 am, and they did their necessary checks, including an ultrasound. The doctor asked, "Do you know that you're pregnant?"

I said "Yes, with twins."

"Well," he said, "they aren't moving." In fact, he only saw one on the monitor, and there was no heartbeat. There was no movement. "Your baby is dead."

I laughed and said, "Okay, cool."

He looked at me confused and said, "What do you mean, 'Okay, cool?'"

I said, "Okay, cool." I put on my clothes and checked out of the hospital. They didn't do anything to stop me.

I went to my gynecologists that same morning. She did another examination and said, "You need to do surgery right away because we don't know how long they have been dead, and anything could happen to your body." Throughout all this, I was not processing the information that was being told to me. I was just moving from one step to the next.

On December 8, 2017, I had surgery to remove twins from my body because they were dead. My body didn't miscarry them; my body was functioning as if it was

15

getting ready to nurture babies, but in my womb, they were dead. I did the surgery and, of course, everyone was disappointed and shocked. I also lost my relationship amid all that. I didn't think about myself in that moment. I bled for about four weeks, and I was busy taking care of everyone else, making sure everyone else was emotionally stable and well. I forgot about me. I forgot to tend to my emotional and psychological wounds; however, I did do all the things I needed to do to physically recover.

One day, pain said hello. One day, when everyone else would have moved on from what had happened a few weeks prior, my journey with this encounter that happened so long ago had just begun. On the day pain said hello—the day pain slapped me in my face and made me realize that I am human; the day pain kicked me in my face and said to me, "You are not worthy." The day pain said to me, "You are a worthless woman." The day pain said to me, "I am going to add depression to your bill." The day pain said to me, "No one cares." I started to spiral out of control, thinking that this was it.

"Where is God when I need Him? Where is my spiritual support when I need them?"

When I thought about it after, I was a bit unfair because no one knew what I went through outside the small circle of people in my family who knew, not even those at my church or those I was close with. I started to blame everyone. I started to blame the world for not knowing, which was kind of silly, but I needed someone to see that I was in pain without me saying that I was in pain. Silly, right? I started church-hopping because of that. I started to withdraw myself from the world but, somehow, still showed up for my functions: work, church, family, friends—I still showed up as if everything was okay, but behind the smile was someone who lost herself. I didn't know if I was going, coming, or staying still. It was just nothingness.

My pain said hello. Trauma took a front seat in the car of my life. The doctor didn't tell me that these things happened. The doctor didn't tell me that it was okay. The doctor didn't tell me that a lot of women go through this. The doctor failed to inform me that a small percentage of women, around 1-5%, encounter a missed miscarriage during their lifetime. Consequently, I felt isolated, believing my pain and experience were unique to me. I questioned my worthiness to continue living.

A missed miscarriage differs from a typical miscarriage as it lacks the usual symptoms of vaginal bleeding and abdominal pain. Instead, the pregnancy halts without any noticeable physical indications. Diagnosis of a missed miscarriage typically relies on ultrasound confirmation, as was the case for me. According to Dr. Susie Kilshaw from U.C.L. Anthropology, approximately 1 in 100 women in the U.K. suffer from recurrent miscarriages, defined as three or more consecutive miscarriages. Moreover, statistics indicate that black women in the U.K. are 43% more likely than white women to experience miscarriages.

You are not alone.

It is not your fault.

There is hope on the other side of hopelessness.

I had to let go of my relationship. He was someone I thought I was going to marry. We were so close, but that is a story for another time. I was aimless, visionless, purposeless, worthless, empty, and dirty because suddenly, I could feel the nothingness in my womb. One minute, there was something there, and I was bonding with them even though I had never met them. I had never seen them fully besides hearing a heartbeat and looking at the size of a raspberry, but the moment I heard the heartbeat, a bond was formed between my babies and me. Now that bond was snatched away from me and left this empty space, a void that escalated to the entirety of how I felt as a woman who could not maintain a relationship or even bring life to life.

God must have made a mistake. Surprisingly in those moments, I didn't turn to sex as a self-soothing mechanism. I felt like I was too unworthy for that. I didn't turn to drugs or alcohol, but I was losing myself within myself. I felt like a little black dot on a large white sheet of paper that couldn't be seen, but I continued to live. I continued to exist without living. I continued to exist without meaning while everyone else carried on with their lives, and the experiences that were shared with them seemed nonexistent. My journey of walking through this unfortunate experience had just begun.

I had to get help; I NEEDED to get help. I started having dreams that would eventually be interpreted as God communicating with me that He was going to deliver me from my pain, and it was time. I remembered that my church offered healing and deliverance sessions. I will share the details of my experience in later chapters. I got an application form, hesitantly filled it out, and submitted it. I also sought the help of a Christian therapist. I needed all of me to be healed. I needed all the help I could get because it was either that or die.

Face the Pain

After four years of navigating this journey, including healing, deliverance, and therapy, I believed I had come

to terms with the pain. I thought I was alright—
enough time had passed. I was actively participating in
various T.V. and radio programs, speaking from the
church altar, and sharing my story on social media. But
then, on Mother's Day, May 10, 2020, I suddenly
broke down. I was still in pain. Healing takes time; I
learned that later.

The most widely accepted definition of pain, according
to the International Association of the Study of Pain,
taken from the National Institute of Health, is this:
"*Pain is an unpleasant sensory and emotional
experience that is associated with actual or potential
tissue damage or described in such terms.*"

I was in a lot of pain. Apparently, I had suffered an
unpleasant sensory and emotional experience that not
only damaged my emotions, but there was actual tissue
damage because of the surgery I had done. One would
think I only had to deal with the pain of the experience,
but there was also trauma that followed. According to
Trauma Informed Implementation Resources Centre,
trauma is defined as a pervasive problem. In other
words, it is an unwanted issue that spreads throughout
your life. It stems from encountering a distressing event
or sequence of occurrences, which could be
emotionally traumatic or life-threatening, causing
persistent negative impacts on a person's overall

functioning and their physical, social, emotional, and/or spiritual well-being.

Dr. Bessel Van Der Kolf, M.D, founder and medical director for the Trauma Centre in his book, "The Body Keeps the Score," puts it this way: *"Trauma leaves traces on our minds and emotions, on our capacity for joy and intimacy, and even on our biology and immune system…Trauma, by definition, is unbearable and intolerable. It takes tremendous energy to keep functioning while carrying the memory of terror, and the shame of utter weakness and vulnerability. While we all want to move beyond trauma, the part of our brain that is devoted to ensuring our survival (deep below our rational brain) is not very good at denial. Long after a traumatic experience is over, it may be reactivated at the slightest hint of danger and mobilize disturbed brain circuits and secrete massive amounts of stress hormones. This precipitates unpleasant emotions, intense physical sensations, and impulsive and aggrieve actions. These posttraumatic reactions feel incomprehensible and overwhelming. Feeling out of control, survivors of trauma often begin to fear that they are damaged to the core and beyond redemption."*

Whew! He sums it right up. I had definitely gone through an experience that left traces on my mind and emotions, causing a disconnect between my reality and what I was feeling inside. It impacted my ability to experience joy and build connections so deeply that the young woman who once eagerly anticipated love and family eventually came to resent them. In 2020, I was now considering removing my tubes (tubal ligation), a procedure that would ensure that I wouldn't be able to have children. When I broke down that day, it felt as though my body was signaling that I still had more healing to do and that there were unresolved layers of pain and trauma. It was clear that I needed to confront this pain head-on.

On that Mother's Day and thereafter, every baby and child I saw would cause a knot in my throat, and a sudden feeling of resentment would begin to surface. Once again, though I seemed to have been functioning and showing up for my different roles as a sister, co-worker, friend, daughter, and girlfriend, something was wrong. I was highly functioning in depression. I was alive but not living; neither was I experiencing fulfillment. This time, apparently, I didn't need more therapy or healing and deliverance sessions. I needed time alone with myself and God on this leg of the journey of healing.

Thankfully, my boss at the time noticed that I was withdrawn, unproductive, and a bit out of it. I spoke to him, and he agreed to allow me to take three months off work. He said, "This job takes mental effort as much as it does physical effort, and if your mind is not in it, it won't work." I took time off and went home to the country. I came off WhatsApp; I was only reachable by regular calls, SMS text messages, or email, which took some adjusting, but I needed to get rid of all distractions as much as possible. I needed to hear from God. I needed to get to know God more. I needed to figure out who this version of me was after having gone through the various sessions I mentioned earlier and now being confronted with additional healing to do and more pain to face. I needed answers. I love basking in nature and being back home in the country provided that outlet. Time to get to work.

Most days, I woke up, had devotions with God, and wrote prayers in the form of letters to God. I found myself searching for God in the Bible, searching for pieces of myself, parts of my story that would help me make sense of what I had gone through and what I was going through. Clearly, God's will for me was not to get a tubal ligation done or for me not to get married. He wanted me to become whole. He wanted me to find love again; love in Him and from Him. I decided to write out all the promises of God that I could find in the Bible and on google that challenged all the negative beliefs I had planted in my mind. I would rewrite them every day and say them out loud as though I was saying affirmations with confirmations, as if I was rewriting my identity, disrupting and confronting the negative

23

self-beliefs I had, and reprograming my mind, body, and brain to accept that rest; what I needed in that season was "productive." Rest is productive.

One of the things my therapist challenged me on was this, "*Who told you that doing nothing was bad? Rest that reset and revitalizes your mental, spiritual, and emotional capacity and brings clarity is productive.*" I started to understand this. I started to understand what it meant to be still while the world continued being hyper-productive and microwave-results-driven. I was facing the pain with stillness, journaling, praying, and talking to God and myself. I learned to literally let go and let God. I let go, trusting that the God who created all things with their purposes and designs had a plan that would work out for my good, even though I stopped showing up in the various places and spaces that required parts of me that I could no longer give. I had to trust that when the time came, and He said it was time to resurface, it would all be well. God is so faithful that when the time did come, the blessings that flowed and how life continued as if I didn't leave was more than I could have ever asked, thought, or imagined (see Ephesians 3:20).

CHAPTER TWO

PEELING BACK THE LAYERS OF HEALING

The healing and deliverance session required me to fill out a questionnaire about eight pages long, back and forth. The questions took me as far back as having to find out if my great-grandparents suffered pain, trauma, mental or spiritual illnesses. It forced me to dig deep and recall even the experience of the person I first had sex with. The session took the form of one three-hour session where my life was spread out bare before the two ministers and ultimately before God. God needed me to lay it all down with witnesses in the mix.

In this chapter, I will share my version of some of the tools that were used for healing and deliverance to take place. This is where we put in some work together to help you on the journey of holistic healing. I found my healing and now know there is hope and faith on the other side. I want to share that with you in this chapter because it does and can get better.

I learned that the real work of healing and deliverance takes place after the session, after you have exposed all of yourself before God with the help of the people He sent to help. I had to learn to maintain my deliverance through self-deliverance. I had to continue to walk out my salvation and sanctification by applying and utilizing the tools given to me daily and continuously renew my mind daily because the enemy never stops reminding you of who you were and what you used to do. The enemy, in this case, is not just the enemy of our spirit—the devil—but also the self-sabotaging enemy (yourself) created from the old version of you, patterns and habits that would want to keep us stuck in a familiar and comfortable partnership which isn't always good. Playing it safe in spaces that feel familiar is not always good, especially when you have grown, have growing to do, and when you are no longer the person your pain and trauma dictated for you to be to survive.

Therapy, healing, and deliverance sessions only work if you are ready and willing to put in the work, even when it gets hard, even when it is painful and uncomfortable. Let's explore some prayer activities you can do to help you begin the journey to face pain and trauma to push the barriers that would eventually reveal your perfect purpose and most authentic self. You are not alone in this; you are partnering with God as you go through these activities. It is important that before you start the other activities that you surrender yourself, mind, body, heart, and the moment to God and, as such, say out loud the surrender prayer below. Give God permission to have His way in that moment and in your life.

The activities included herein were inspired by my experience of restoring the foundations ministry as well as now being a team member of the healing and deliverance ministry at my church. Surprise! I did make it to the other side. I can now help you find healing, deliverance, and freedom as I did.

The Power of Surrender: Opening Yourself for Healing

Let's be honest: having control of ourselves and everything around us can feel so good sometimes, and being told that we must surrender, especially to God so we can have more of Him, makes us cringe. Another truth is that there is power in your surrender. The Word of God says in Matthew 16: 24-25, *"Then Jesus said to His disciples, "if anyone desires to come after Me, let him deny himself, and take up his cross, and follow Me. For whoever desires to save his life will lose it, but whoever loses his life for My sake will find it."*

(KJV). I believe a lot of us get stuck in the "deny himself" part of the instruction because we are fearful of the unknown, not knowing who we are without our pain, trauma, and baggage. We like control. It took coming to the edge of losing myself after that loss to realize that I had to let go and let God because the opposite of what the pain from this hurt required of me to do was too unbearable. There must be a reason for this; there must be a solution.

I was emotionally, physically, and psychologically tired. I had nothing left but the small and subtle voice of what I thought to be the voice of God at the time, telling me to let Him in. In the scripture above, I found the first prescription to my pain, and I want to share it with you. I know it is hard; however, from one overcomer to the next, it is worth it.

Keep going.

The second prescription I found that would allow me to activate the power within me to surrender was in Matthew 11:28-29, *"Come to me, all you who are weary and burdened, and I will give you rest. Take my yoke upon you and learn from me, for I am gentle and humble in heart, and you will find rest for your souls."* *(KJV)*. It was okay to surrender because there was rest to be found for my weary and burdened soul, and believe me, I was so tired from the pain of losing so much, and no one seemed to understand, or so I thought. I needed to find out what it meant to completely surrender and rest. After all, I didn't know what else to do. This was my last chance at life.

If you can relate to all of that, then this part is for you. Say the prayer below out loud with meaning. Say it like you want to release that pain. Say it like you have had enough!

Dear Lord,

I humbly seek Your help as I engage in this prayer for healing and deliverance. Please bring healing, deliverance, and renewed hope into my life. I am grateful for Your unconditional love and acceptance, and I acknowledge my need for growth and change.

I take responsibility for my actions and ask You to reveal any areas where I've been blind. I confess my sins and those of my ancestors, releasing them from blame and renouncing their effects on my life through Christ's sacrifice.

I break the power of curses and demonic oppression stemming from ancestral sins. I declare my allegiance to Jesus Christ and cancel any influence from past dedications.

Thank You for revealing the lies I've believed and for empowering me to renew my mind. Please heal the pain I've held onto and help me discern any misplaced blame.

You are my deliverer, Lord. Free me from every stronghold and grant me the authority to walk in freedom. Holy Spirit, guide me in truth and provide comfort.

In Jesus' name. Amen.

Take a deep breath. Inhale through your nose for four seconds, hold for four seconds, and slowly release (exhale) through your mouth for four seconds.

You are safe.
You are okay.
You are loved.

You are seen.

Let's go deeper.

Journal prompt: Make a list of all the things you are surrendering. Feel yourself release them as you write each item out.

I am proud of you. Now keep going.

Breaking Generational Curses

To get the desired healing I was craving, I had to dig deep. I had to unclutter beliefs and curses that were spoken over my life by myself and any I had accepted spoken by others because of the pain and trauma from losing twins and that relationship. I also had to face those that were spoken over and through my family that would have been passed down to me before I was even born.

Some of your struggles and maladaptive cycles didn't start with you. They were imprinted and passed down from your parents or generations before them that were accepted over time, and no one bothered to break the cycle, or they perhaps didn't know they could or knew how to. This is your chance to stop that cycle and allow healing to start with you and the generations that will come after you. I had to confront curses such as the belief that I would always be alone (abandonment), I would not be able to have children, or that I would not amount to anything (worthlessness) by using the prayer strategy below. If God spoke the world into existence, it means that words are powerful, and we were made in His image and likeness. Therefore, even as you repeat this prayer, don't underestimate the effect it can and will have by you speaking it out loud to God and to yourself. Feel free to go over this as many times as you need to.

Prayer:

> *I acknowledge and confess the sins of my ancestors, parents, and my own transgressions. I willingly extend forgiveness to my ancestors and all others who have influenced me, releasing them from the burden of these sins and their repercussions in my life.*

Lord, I ask for Your forgiveness for my own actions and for succumbing to these curses. I accept Your forgiveness, and based on it, I forgive myself for falling into these sins. I reject these sins and curses, breaking their hold over my life and the lives of my descendants through the redemptive sacrifice of Christ on the cross. I embrace God's liberation from these sins and their consequences, welcoming healing, peace, deliverance, and freedom from pain and trauma through Your grace and mercy. In Jesus' name. Amen.

Take a deep breath, inhale through your nose for four seconds, hold for four seconds, and slowly release (exhale) through your mouth for four seconds.

You are safe.
You are okay.
You are loved.

You are seen. Let's go deeper.

Liberating Past Chains and Ungodly Soul Ties

On my journey to healing, freedom, and deliverance, I needed to cut all emotional, spiritual, and sexual soul ties with anyone in my past who had a negative influence over my life and all the decisions I made at that time that were opposite to the word, nature, and character of God.

Soul ties are emotional and spiritual connections between two or more people formed through relationships and interactions with friends, romantic partners, items, family members, and co-workers. These connections would have had some influence or control over your life, and the decisions you made at some point or another led to a path that had nothing to do with God. Neither did they have any positive influence over your life. You need to be liberated from them.

I had to dig deep. I was challenged to make a list of all the people I had emotional entanglement, spiritual, and sexual encounters with. Yikes! I know. We are laying it all down, getting completely uncovered before God and ourselves. This step is necessary for the new fertile ground we are trying to create so that the healthy and fruitful godly seeds we plant at the end of this book can find good ground to grow purposefully and intentionally and produce healthy fruits.

Read the prayer below out loud and be honest with yourself and God. After all, you can't hide anything from Him that He doesn't already know. It is interesting how we try to layer ourselves with so many masks before the one who created us. He knew us before we were conceived and know the exact number of hairs on our heads, yet we still try to hide our dirt as if God is another human being.

Prayer prompt:

> Father, I come to You in no other name but the name of Your Son, Jesus Christ, the redeemer of my journey in this life. The one who is more than capable of wiping my slate clean and giving me a fresh start. Forgive me, Father, for putting _____ [insert the name of each person here] before You and allowing him/her to override Your guidance and influence in my life. I uproot and release myself from all the ways _____ [insert the name of each person here] has influenced me to sin against You by forming emotional, spiritual, and sexual soul ties. I admit to having unhealthy emotional and spiritual connections with [name]. I forgive [name] for their involvement in these connections. Lord, forgive me for my part in these ties. I reject and sever each unhealthy connection. I free myself from the influence of each person named. I reject and nullify any influences associated with these ties.

Take a deep breath through your nose, hold it for four seconds, then exhale through your mouth slowly. You are going to get through this.

Let's go deeper.

Embracing Forgiveness as a Key to Inner Restoration

We are often told that forgiveness is not for the other person, it is for us, and it is true. Withholding forgiveness is like feeding yourself poison while you wait for the other person who hurt you to die from it. Imagine you holding on to all that unforgiveness while you watch the person who may have done you wrong continue to live and enjoy their life. Don't you want to be free? In my own journey that I shared in the beginning of this book, I had to learn to forgive my ex, God and, most importantly, myself.

One night after finishing a live interview on Instagram, God said to me, "*How will they know that undiluted and unconditional forgiveness is possible if you don't allow Me to show you how to forgive? How will they know and feel that My love is free and real? Unblock your ex and pray for his union and his wife!*" LISTEN! As the song said, "*Putting up a resistance*"; I absolutely resisted initially, but I couldn't fight the instructions God had given, so I did what I was asked to do. I unblocked him and sent a six-minute voice note of me just allowing the Holy Spirit to pray. Interestingly, the following week, a church reached out to me to speak on the topic of forgiveness. God has a big sense of humor.

Most of the time, if we are being honest, we practice lip service by saying, "I forgive you," without actually forgiving the person in our hearts. We still can't stand to be around them, hear about them, or even see them, and if God sends you on an assignment to either deliver a message or pray for them, you can't. This is when you are tested to see if you have truly forgiven a person from the heart and not just repeating the words because they sound mature and cute. Every fruit you proclaim to portray/represent will be tested and strengthened.

Unforgiveness can literally be converted in your body as stress and cause your body to hold it in, which later presents itself as uneasiness. It can lead to insomnia and headaches caused by overthinking and anxiety that affects all other areas of your life, and then you wonder why. It is time to let it go; let them go and be free.

Trauma, as I mentioned in the previous chapter, leaves traces that completely dysregulate your well-being physically, emotionally, and spiritually.

Repeat this prayer out loud. It is important that you hear yourself proclaim with authority the words coming from your mouth.

> *Father, You desire healing and freedom for me through forgiveness. I choose to forgive [name] for [specific actions]. I forgive those who led me into sin and hurt me from their own pain. I release them from any debt I thought they owed me and let go of judgments and desires for punishment. I surrender them to You, in Jesus' name. Amen.*

Self-Forgiveness

> *Father, because You've forgiven me, I forgive myself for hurting others and myself. I release myself from self-condemnation, judgments, and hatred. I forgive my mistakes and shortcomings, accepting myself as You do. With Your help, I'll learn to love myself, knowing You're guiding me forward. Holy Spirit, sanctify me and shape me into Christ's image. In Jesus' name. Amen.*

Take a deep breath, inhale for four seconds, hold for four seconds, and then release (exhale) for four seconds.

You are safe.

You are okay.
You are loved.
You are seen.

Silencing Word Curses

In Proverbs 18:21, we learn that life and death are in the power of the tongue, and those who love it will eat its fruits. Sometimes we say and affirm some things over our lives and that of others—even in jests—without realizing we are literally arming the enemy with bullets to open doors to bring death, purposelessness, chaos, and destruction into our lives. It is not the same day a seed is planted, whether by God or the enemy or yourself, that the fruit is produced. Growth, even if that growth is meant to destroy us, takes time. Be careful and cautious of the words that come out of your mouth or the words that come out of others' mouths when they say bad things about your life or things that are not a blessing over your life. The same mouth that is used to pronounce favor and blessing can be used to declare curses and destruction.

Below are examples of word curses. If you remember more than one instance where either you or someone else made such statements and you agreed with them without rejecting or counteracting them, then the following prayer is for you.

Tick as many of the word curses that you can relate to below. Fill in the last two with any that crossed your mind.

I/you will never be successful.	I/you were born to suffer.	I/you won't be able to have kids.
I/you are not as good as…	You'll always struggle with money	I/you are better off dead.
This drives me crazy, or I am crazy.	I am so dumb/You are so dumb.	I am probably going to end up _____, just like my mother/father.
I always get sick every Christmas, New Year, Birthday, etc.	I am so lazy/you are so lazy.	I/you will never get a job.
I/you have the worst luck.	I/you are such a failure.	Nobody will ever want to marry me/you.
People will always use me.	All men want from me is sex.	I will never be able to accomplish this…
I will always be late.	I will fail if I try.	I cannot trust men.

I/you will never change; this cycle will always continue.	Nothing ever goes right for you.	

Repeat the prayer prompt below as many times as you need to.

Prayer Prompt

> *I forgive [myself or anyone else that comes to mind] for speaking curses over me, like saying "I'm not good enough." [Feel free to adjust with your own words.] I repent for allowing these curses to affect me.*

> *Lord, forgive me. I accept Your forgiveness. I reject and break the power of these curses in my life through Jesus' sacrifice on the cross. I use His authority to cancel their influence and dismantle any strongholds they've created.*

Harnessing the Power of Positive Affirmations

Now that we have learned how powerful words are, we can now form positive affirmations. For days, I wrote over the same twenty affirmations, and then I would repeat them to myself repeatedly. These affirmations were also God's promises written over as affirmations.

This was also my attempt at renewing my mind. I was on a mission to rewire my brain and how I felt about myself, my life, the people in it, and God. I was tired of stinking-thinking and the thoughts the trauma dictated that I should have. It is not good enough to just repeat and affirm these words; it is important that you also practice them when the tests and trials of life come; they WILL come.

Here are a few positive affirmations that you could start with on your journey to healing:

- I am so happy and grateful that the joy of the Lord is my strength.
- I am so happy and grateful that I am successful at my job; I am winning.
- I am so happy and grateful that I have overcome negative thinking, depression, and the battlefield in my mind.
- I am so happy and grateful that I am at peace.
- I am so happy and grateful that my relationship with God has been strengthened.
- I am so happy and grateful that I am operating in God's purpose for my life. Everything I do, I prosper.
- I am so happy and grateful that I am walking in God's favor and abundance.

- I am so happy and grateful that God-directed doors of opportunities have opened for me.
- I am so happy and grateful that I have a strong support system of God-fearing friends.
- I am a lean, mean money-making machine. Money knows my name; money finds me now, and it flows to me with ease.

Additionally, having created your affirmations, I challenge you to create a personal vision statement for yourself. This statement describes your goals, strengths, and personal values. It can be focused on your personal life or professional goals. The intention of this is to keep you focused in those moments when the doubts of life become a bit too loud. The personal vision statement helps you stay focused and move forward toward your long-term vision personally and professionally.

Write out the statement, put it on your bathroom or kitchen wall, or save it as a phone screen wallpaper picture to have as a constant reminder when you need it the most.

Here is an example of a personal vision statement below:

"I am_____ [your name], a passionate and dedicated individual committed to lifelong learning and personal growth. My vision is to create a positive impact in my community and the world through compassion, innovation, and leadership. I strive to inspire and empower others by sharing knowledge, fostering inclusive environments, and championing sustainable practices. My ultimate goal is to lead a fulfilling life characterized by integrity, resilience, and a deep sense of purpose, continually striving to make a meaningful difference in the lives of those around me."

Overcoming Ungodly Beliefs

At some point along my journey, I had built up a wall of resentment towards God, and I engraved some limiting beliefs about Him in my heart. *"How could You allow me to go through what I had gone through? I guess You don't care about me enough to save me?"* were questions I kept asking Him. I realized that to move forward, I had to set the record straight and uproot any ungodly beliefs I had that did not line up with the Word of God or His character. I realized too that our choices come with consequences. Whether we pay the bill for them immediately or later, we will face the consequences of our choices, which has nothing to do with God. His promise in those instances when I was being selfish and stubborn, was that no matter the choices I made, especially when I didn't take the warnings after He showed me what was coming in the dreams I had, was that through it all, and in the end, He WILL always work things out for my good so that He gets the glory. That is exactly what He did and continues to do.

Remember, words are extremely powerful. Repeat this prayer out loud as many times as you feel the need to.

Dear God,

I come before You with an open heart, seeking healing and transformation from the ungodly beliefs that have bound me. I acknowledge that these beliefs have kept me shackled, preventing me from fully embracing the truth of Your love and grace.

I ask for Your guidance and strength as I embark on this journey of overcoming ungodly beliefs. Help me to recognize these falsehoods for what they are and to replace them with the truth of Your Word.

Grant me the courage to confront the lies that have taken root in my heart and mind. Fill me

45

with Your Holy Spirit, illuminating the path to healing and restoration.

May Your truth penetrate every fiber of my being, dispelling darkness and bringing forth light. Help me to fully embrace the truth of who You are and who I am in You.

In Jesus' name. Amen.

Breathe.

Take a deep breath through your nose for four seconds, hold for four seconds, and breathe out through your mouth as slowly as you can count to four.

I am so proud of you!

Below are some practical steps that I found useful on my journey to overcoming ungodly beliefs by embracing the truth in God's Word:

1. **Daily Scripture Reading and Meditation:** Set aside time each day to read and reflect on passages of scripture that speak to God's love, grace, and truth. Allow His Word to penetrate your heart and mind, replacing ungodly beliefs with His eternal truths. An effective method I found useful when reading the scripture was the

S.O.A.P. method developed by Pastor Wayne Cordeiro.

Scripture: Read a short Bible passage out loud and/or write it out.

Observation: Ask the holy Spirit what He wants you to notice about the verses. What do you think the main message is? What verses, words, or ideas jump out to you?

Application: Ask God how He wants you to apply the verse to your own life.

Prayer: Pray for yourself and/or for others.

2. **Journaling:** Keep a journal to record your thoughts, emotions, and experiences as you confront ungodly beliefs and embrace truth. Writing can be a powerful tool for self-reflection and growth, allowing you to track your progress and identify patterns of thought that need to be addressed over time. It is a process and a journey; be patient.

3. **Affirmations:** Create affirmations based on biblical truths that counteract ungodly beliefs. You can refer to the ones you created in the previous chapter. Repeat these affirmations

47

daily, affirming your identity and worth in Christ. For example, *"I am fearfully and wonderfully made"* (see Psalm 139:14) can counteract feelings of inadequacy or unworthiness.

4. **Seek Accountability and Support:** Surround yourself with supportive individuals who can encourage and uplift you on your journey toward healing and truth. Share your struggles and victories with trusted friends, mentors, or counselors who can provide guidance and accountability.

5. **Practice Gratitude:** Cultivate a spirit of gratitude by intentionally focusing on the blessings in your life. Keep a gratitude journal or simply take time each day to thank God for His goodness and faithfulness. Gratitude shifts your perspective from negativity to positivity, helping to combat ungodly beliefs with a mindset of abundance and joy.

Embracing Truth for Healing

Let's be real: there is no way you can heal from something you refuse to confess or admit. It is like having a deep cut; to heal it, you must go through the process of uncovering the scabs and dead flesh to treat it very often until, eventually, what once hurt like hell becomes only a scar with memories to look back on how far you have come since that incident happened.

Embracing truth is a fundamental step toward genuine healing, whether it pertains to emotional wounds, psychological struggles, or physical ailments. The journey toward healing begins with the acknowledgment of reality as it is, not as we wish it to be. This acceptance is neither passive resignation nor an excuse for inaction; rather, it is an active and courageous stance that forms the bedrock of personal growth and transformation, and, to be honest, I couldn't have faced my truths without the help and guidance of the Holy Spirit. A relationship with God on this journey of healing is highly important.

When we embrace the truth, we open ourselves up to a deeper understanding of our circumstances and the root causes of our suffering. This clarity is essential for effective healing. In the realm of emotional and psychological health, for instance, confronting painful memories, unacknowledged feelings, and suppressed trauma is crucial. Through this confrontation, we begin to dismantle the power these hidden truths hold over us. By acknowledging our pain, we can start to work through it, finding ways to integrate our experiences into a coherent and healthier sense of self.

Moreover, embracing truth fosters authenticity. In a world that often encourages masks and facades, living authentically can be revolutionary. Authenticity involves being honest with ourselves and others about who we are, what we feel, and what we need. This honesty can lead to deeper and more meaningful relationships as it removes the barriers that dishonesty and pretense erect. It allows others to connect with us on a genuine level, fostering empathy and support that are vital for healing.

When it comes to physical health, for example, embracing truth means acknowledging the realities of our bodies and their limitations. This might involve accepting a diagnosis, recognizing the impact of lifestyle choices, or admitting the need for help. Denial and avoidance can lead to worsening conditions and missed opportunities for early intervention and effective treatment. Conversely, facing the truth can lead to proactive health management, better coping strategies, and a greater quality of life.

The process of embracing truth is not without its challenges. It requires courage to face uncomfortable realities, and vulnerability to admit our weaknesses and mistakes. However, through this very process, we find strength and resilience. By confronting and accepting our truths, we can begin to let go of shame, guilt, and denial, replacing them with self-compassion and a proactive approach to healing.

Truth acts as a compass, guiding us toward decisions that are in alignment with our true selves, which is who God created us to be and our genuine needs. It helps us set realistic goals, make informed choices, and pursue paths that lead to long-term well-being rather than short-term relief. This alignment with truth ensures that our efforts in healing are effective and sustainable.

Embracing truth is a powerful catalyst for healing. It allows us to confront and process our pain, live authentically, and make informed decisions about our health and well-being. While it requires courage and vulnerability, the rewards are profound: a life characterized by authenticity, resilience, and genuine connection with us and others. By embracing truth, we set the stage for profound and lasting healing.

What are some hard truths that you need to confess for God to begin His work so you can move forward freely?

What are you holding on to that God has been asking you to let go of so that you can receive what He has been trying to give you?

Sealing the Deal

Pain and trauma are profound experiences that can shatter one's sense of security and well-being. What I went through did that. However, within these difficult experiences lies the potential for transformation and purpose. "Sealing the Deal" at this point in the journey means reaching a pivotal point where we recognize and harness the lessons and strength derived from our suffering, thus discovering a deeper purpose that transcends the pain, deciding that it is time for trauma and its effects to take a back seat.

The first step in this journey is acceptance. Pain and trauma often leave us grappling with a sense of injustice or confusion. By accepting the reality of our experiences, we stop resisting the pain and start exploring its depths. This doesn't mean condoning what happened but acknowledging its impact on our lives. Acceptance allows us to begin the process of healing by giving ourselves permission to feel and understand our emotions fully.

From acceptance, we move toward introspection. Reflecting on our pain helps us uncover the hidden narratives and beliefs that shape our responses. This self-examination is crucial for identifying patterns that may be hindering our growth. For instance, trauma can instill a sense of helplessness or unworthiness. By confronting these internalized beliefs, we can start to challenge and change them, paving the way for personal empowerment.

A significant aspect of sealing the deal is finding meaning in our pain. Viktor Frankl, a renowned psychiatrist and Holocaust survivor, emphasized the importance of meaning in his work. He argued that finding purpose in suffering is essential for psychological resilience. This purpose doesn't have to be grandiose; it can be as simple as using our experiences to foster empathy and support for others going through similar challenges. Transforming personal pain into a source of strength and compassion can be profoundly healing.

Another vital element is the power of narrative. Sharing our stories with others lightens the burden of carrying pain alone and connects us with a community of understanding and support. This collective healing can be a source of profound strength and inspiration. When we share our journeys, we validate our experiences and inspire others to find their own purpose in pain. As reluctant as I was when God told me to begin to share my journey about the missed miscarriage, I had to do it; otherwise, I wouldn't be here now sharing this journey with you. There is strength and healing in vulnerability and community.

Growth through trauma often leads to the development of resilience and a renewed sense of purpose. Resilience is not just about bouncing back; it is about growing through adversity and emerging stronger. This growth can lead us to discover new passions, career paths, or creative outlets that we might have never considered otherwise. Many individuals find that their pain becomes a catalyst for advocacy, artistic expression, or other forms of contribution to society.

To truly seal the deal, it is essential to commit to ongoing self-care and personal development, and, of course, by now you should know that there is no self-care without personal development with God and nurturing your relationship with Him. Healing is not a one-time event but a continuous process. Regular practices such as mindfulness, therapy, journaling, and connecting with supportive communities can help maintain our progress and keep us aligned with our newfound purpose.

Sealing the deal for discovering the perfect purpose in pain and trauma involves accepting our experiences, introspecting to understand their impact, finding meaning in our suffering, sharing our stories, and committing to continuous growth. By transforming our pain into purpose, we not only heal ourselves but also contribute positively to the world around us. This transformation is the ultimate testament to the human spirit's capacity for resilience and renewal.

CHAPTER THREE

GOD'S PERFECT PURPOSE: THE TURNING POINT

In the end, having gone through all that I have shared with you, I did discover God's perfect purpose for my life. In fact, I am living it out right now. A part of that journey involves sharing this book with you.

Additionally, as I mentioned in a previous chapter, I am a team member of the healing and deliverance ministry at church. I left my corporate job to fully pursue purpose and passion while monetizing the gifts that were given to me by starting my own registered business known as C.K.M. Healing Consultancy, where, with a little care, we ignite the mind for healing while reaching people who are broken to inspire hope in their lives. I am a trained Trauma Informed Consultant, a Christian Life Coach and so much more, all while using the gifts that God gave me.

All this time, through the confusion, pain, trauma, uncertainty, and refining and re-finding my identity, God was working out everything for my good so that He would get the glory of it all. I am content with why God made me. I am content with who I am, and I continue to practice healing and deliverance. I continue to unlearn and relearn the various versions of myself that show up in the various seasons of life, as Michelle Obama said in her book "Becoming": *"For me, becoming isn't about arriving somewhere or achieving a certain aim. I see it instead as forward motion, a means of evolving, a way to reach continuously toward a better self. The journey doesn't end. Do we settle for the world as it is, or do we work for the world as it should be?"*

The journey of peeling back the layers of healing is continuous because we heal in layers, not all at once. It becomes a bit easier when your foundation has been restored. You must use the firm foundation of Jesus Christ to reclaim the territories of your life you can control. Take a Chief Operating Officer approach to your own life while believing that you deserve good things, including that perfect peace that surpasses all understanding that God talks about.

CONCLUSION

I want you to know that there is hope on the other side of your pain. There is freedom that can be found on the other side of that fear and there is divine joy that can be discovered because of facing your pain and trauma.

You can connect with me on YouTube at Trauma Talks with C.K.M.H.C.; your gateway to exploring the multifaceted realm of trauma. Join us as we dive into its definitions, dispel myths, unveil the staggering statistics linking unaddressed trauma to lifestyle diseases, and empower you with actionable insights.

I am also on Instagram and Facebook at C.K.M. Healing Consultancy or Chantaeu Munroe. You can also connect with me via email at ckmhealingconsutlancy@gmail.com, call us at (876) 455-9481, or visit our website at ckmconsultancyja.com to find out ways you can book our services to journey with us as you face the pain and begin your journey of healing.

ABOUT THE AUTHOR

Chantaeu Munroe is a colorful individual, defined by the layers that constitute her essence—where beauty, chaos, wonder, and adventure intertwine. She serves as a Christian Life Coach, a Certified Clinical Trauma Professional, a team member of the Healing and

Deliverance Ministry, and holds the role of C.E.O. and founder at C.K.M. Healing Consultancy.

At C.K.M. Healing Consultancy, the belief is rooted in the transformative power of holistic healing for the mind and body, guided by the Holy Spirit's influence.

Made in the USA
Columbia, SC
29 October 2024

44990824R00035